Table of Contents

Welcome to ACA

Welcome to the ACA program. This is a Twelve Step, Twelve Traditio support group focused on understanding the specific behavior and attitud patterns we developed while growing up in an alcoholic or other dysfunction environment. These patterns continue to affect us today.

By attending regular meetings we come to a better understanding of our pa so we can more effectively restructure our lives today. We begin to see mo clearly what is positive and healthy in ourselves.

ACA is not a replacement for addicts working an abstinence program in oth Twelve Step fellowships. However, Adult Children of Alcoholics is often th only program for many adult children recovering from the effects of alcoholis or other family dysfunction, including the effects of alcoholism and dru addiction. (Adapted from the ACA Fellowship textbook.)

Meetings are intended to be safe places where we can share our experienc strength and hope without judgment or criticism. We have the right not share unless we are ready.

This program is grounded in spiritual guidance and not affiliated with a specific religion. We are individuals struggling through rigorous honesty become the best we can be. We respect one another's anonymity. Who v encounter at meetings and what they have said there is treated confidentially

We meet together to share our experience, strength, hope and fear; we off friendship and understanding. We love one another in a very special way. W welcome you to join us.

Since each meeting is autonomous, and each meeting is a differe experience, we recommend that you try as many different ones as possib before deciding if the ACA program can be helpful to you in your journe from discovery to recovery.

Keep coming back.

"The Laundry List"
(14 Traits of an Adult Child)

1. We became isolated and afraid of people and authority figures.

2. We became approval seekers and lost our identity in the process.

3. We are frightened by angry people and any personal criticism.

4. We either become alcoholics, marry them or both, or find another compulsive personality such as a workaholic to fulfill our sick abandonment needs.

5. We live life from the viewpoint of victims and are attracted by that weakness in our love and friendship relationships.

6. We have an overdeveloped sense of responsibility, and it is easier for us to be concerned with others rather than ourselves; this enables us not to look too closely at our own faults, etc.

7. We get guilt feelings when we stand up for ourselves instead of giving in to others.

8. We became addicted to excitement.

9. We confuse love and pity and tend to "love" people we can "pity" and "rescue."

10. We have "stuffed" our feelings from our traumatic childhoods and have lost the ability to feel or express our feelings because it hurts so much (Denial).

11. We judge ourselves harshly and have a very low sense of self-esteem.

12. We are dependent personalities who are terrified of abandonment and will do anything to hold on to a relationship in order not to experience painful abandonment feelings, which we received from living with sick people who were never there emotionally for us.

13. Alcoholism is a family disease; we became para-alcoholics and took on the characteristics of that disease even though we did not pick up the drink.

14. Para-alcoholics are reactors rather than actors.

Tony A.
1978

Am I an Adult Child?

1.   Do you recall anyone drinking or taking drugs or being involved in some other behavior you now consider dysfunctional?

2.   Did you avoid bringing friends to your home because of drinking or some other dysfunctional behavior in the home?

3.   Did one of your parents make excuses for the other parent's drinking or other behavior?

4.   Did your parents focus on each other so much that they seemed to ignore you?

5.   Did your parents or relatives argue constantly?

6.   Were you drawn into arguments or disagreements and asked to choose sides with one parent or relative against another?

7.   Did you try to protect your brothers or sisters against drinking or other behavior in the family?

8.   As an adult, do you feel immature? Do you feel like you are a child inside?

9.   As an adult, do you believe you are treated like a child when you interact with your parents? Are you continuing to live out a childhood role with the parents?

10. Do you believe that it is your responsibility to take care of the parents' feelings or worries? Do other relatives look to you to solve their problems?

11. Do you fear authority figures and angry people?

12. Do you constantly seek approval or praise but have difficulty accepting a compliment when one comes your way?

13. Do you see most forms of personal criticism as an attack?

14. Do you over commit yourself and then feel angry when others do not appreciate what you do?

15. Do you think you are responsible for the way another person feels or behaves?

16. Do you have difficulty identifying feelings?

17. Do you focus outside yourself for love or security?

18. Do you involve yourself in the problems of others? Do you feel more alive when there is a crisis?

19. Do you equate sex with intimacy?

20. Do you confuse love and pity?

21. Have you found yourself in a relationship with a compulsive or dangerous person and wondered how you got there?

22. Do you judge yourself without mercy and guess at what is normal?

23. Do you behave one way in public and another way at home?

24. Do you think your parents had a problem with drinking or taking drugs?

25. Do you think you were affected by the drinking or other dysfunctional behavior of your parents or family?

If you answered *yes* to three or more of these questions, you may be suffering from the effects of growing up in an alcoholic or other dysfunctional family.

ACA Fellowship Text, pp. 18–20
© *Adult Children of Alcoholics®/Dysfunctional Families*
World Service Organization

The ACA Program and How it Works

We find that a difference in identity and purpose distinguishes Adult Childre
of Alcoholics from other Twelve Step Programs and underscores the need for ou
special focus.

Characteristics

The central problems for ACAs is a mistaken belief, formed in childhooc
which affects every part of our lives. As children, we fought to survive th
destructive effects of alcoholism, and began an endless struggle to change
troubled dysfunctional family into a loving, supportive one. We reach adulthooc
believing we failed, unable to see that no one can stop the traumatic effects o
family alcoholism.

Following naturally from this pervasive sense of failure are self-blame, sham
and guilt. These self-accusations ultimately lead to self-hate. Accepting ou
basic powerlessness to control alcoholic behavior and its effect on the famil
is the key that unlocks the Inner Child and lets reparenting begin. The "Firs
Step" is applied to family alcoholism; a fundamental basis for self-hate n
longer exists.

The ACA Program

Two characteristics identify the ACA Program. The program is for adult
raised in alcoholic homes, and although substance abuse may exist, the focus i
on the *self*, specifically on reaching and freeing the Inner Child, hidden behin
a protective shield of denial.

The purpose of ACA is threefold – to shelter and support "newcomers" i
confronting "denial;" to comfort those mourning their early loss of securit
trust and love; and to teach the skills for reparenting ourselves with gentlenes
humor, love and respect.

Recovery in ACA

Moving from isolation is the first step an Adult Child makes in recoverin
the self. Isolation is both a prison and a sanctuary. Adult Children, suspende
between need and fear – unable to choose between fight or flight – agoniz
in the middle and resolve the tension by explosive bursts of rebellion, or b
silently enduring the despair. Isolation is our retreat from the paralyzing pai
of indecision.

his retreat into denial blunts our awareness of the destructive reality of family lcoholism and the first stage of mourning and grief. It allows us to cope with 1e loss of love and to survive in the face of neglect and abuse.

he return of feelings is the second stage of mourning and indicates healing as begun. Initial feelings of anger, guilt, rage and despair resolve into a final cceptance of loss. Genuine grieving for our childhood ends our morbid ascination with the past and lets us return to the present, free to live as adults. 'onfronting years of pain and loss at first seems overwhelming. Jim Goodwin, 1 describing the post-traumatic stress of Vietnam veterans, writes that some eterans, "...actually believe that if they once again allow themselves to feel, 1ey may never stop crying or may completely lose control...."[1,2]

haring the burden of grief others feel gives us the courage and strength to ace our own bereavement. The pain of mourning and grief is balanced by being ble, once again, to fully love and care for someone and to freely experience >y in life.

Reparenting Ourselves

he need to reparent ourselves comes from our efforts to feel safe as children. he violent nature of alcoholism darkened our emotional world and left us ounded, hurt and unable to feel. This extreme alienation from our own internal irection kept us helplessly dependent on those we mistrusted and feared.

1 an unstable, hostile, and often dangerous environment, we attempted to meet 1e impossible demands of living with family alcoholism, and our lives were >on out of control. To make sense of the confusion, and to end our feelings f fear, we denied inconsistencies in what we were taught. We held rigidly to a :w certain beliefs, or we rebelled and distrusted all outside interference.

reedom begins with being open to love. The dilemma of abandonment is a 1oice between painful intimacy or hopeless isolation, but the consequence is 1e same – we protect ourselves by rejecting the vulnerable Inner Child and are >rced to live without warmth or love. Without love, intimacy and isolation are qually painful, empty and incomplete.

ove dissolves hate. We give ourselves the love we need by releasing our self-atred and embracing the child inside. With a child's sensitivity, we reach ut to explore the world again and become aware of the need to trust and >ve others.

"The Etiology of Combat-Related Post-Traumatic Stress Disorders"

Post traumatic stress is the tension of unresolved grief following the loss of fundamental security.

The warm affection we have for each other heals our inner hurt. ACA loving acceptance and gentle support lessen our feelings of fear. We share ou beliefs and mistrust without judgment or criticism. We realize the insanity alcoholism and become willing to replace the confusing beliefs of childhoc with the clear, consistent direction of the Twelve Steps and Twelve Tradition and to accept the authority of the loving God they reflect.

ACA is a Twelve Step Program of Recovery

ACA's relationship to other anonymous programs is a shared dependence the Twelve Steps for a spiritual awakening. Each program's focus is differe but the solution remains the same.

In childhood our identity is formed by the reflection we see in the eyes of th people around us. We fear losing this reflection – thinking the mirror makes real and that we disappear or have no self without it.

The distorted image of family alcoholism is not who we are. And we are not th unreal person trying to mask that distortion. In ACA we do not stop abusir a substance, or stop losing ourselves in another. We stop believing we have worth and we start to see our true identity, reflected in the eyes of other Adu Children, as the strong survivors and valuable people we actually are.

NOTE: ACA literature has been updated to include "dysfunctional family" where at all possible. T *Identity Papers* were copyrighted prior to this decision. It is understood there are other causes dysfunctional behavior.

The Problem

Many of us found that we had several characteristics in common as a result of being brought up in an alcoholic or other dysfunctional household. We had come to feel isolated, and uneasy with other people—especially with authority figures. To protect ourselves, we became people-pleasers, even though we lost our own identities in the process. All the same we would mistake any personal criticism as a threat. We either became alcoholics (or practiced other addictive behavior) ourselves, or married them, or both. Failing that, we found other compulsive personalities, such as a workaholic, to fulfill our sick need for abandonment.

We lived life from the standpoint of victims. Having an overdeveloped sense of responsibility, we preferred to be concerned with others rather than ourselves. We got guilt feelings when we stood up for ourselves rather than giving in to others. Thus we became reactors rather than actors, letting others take the initiative. We were dependent personalities, terrified of abandonment, willing to do almost anything to hold on to a relationship in order not to be abandoned emotionally. Yet we kept choosing insecure relationships because they matched our childhood relationship with alcoholic or dysfunctional parents.

These symptoms of the family disease of alcoholism or other dysfunction made us "co-victims," those who take on the characteristics of the disease without necessarily ever taking a drink. We learned to keep our feelings down as children and kept them buried as adults. As a result of this conditioning, we confused love with pity, tending to love those we could rescue. Even more self-defeating, we became addicted to excitement in all our affairs, preferring constant upset to workable relationships. This is a description, not an indictment.

The Solution

The solution is to become your own loving parent.

As ACA becomes a safe place for you, you will find freedom to express all the hurts and fears that you have kept inside and to free yourself from the shame and blame that are carryovers from the past. You will become an adult who is imprisoned no longer by childhood reactions. You will recover the child within you, learning to love and accept yourself.

The healing begins when we risk moving out of isolation. Feelings and buried memories will return. By gradually releasing the burden of unexpressed grief, we slowly move out of the past. We learn to reparent ourselves with gentleness, humor, love and respect.

This process allows us to see our biological parents as the instruments of our existence. Our actual parent is a Higher Power whom some of us choose to call God. Although we had alcoholic or dysfunctional parents, our Higher Power gave us the Twelve Steps of recovery.

This is the action and work that heals us: we use the Steps; we use the meetings; we use the telephone. We share our experience, strength, and hope with each other. We learn to restructure our sick thinking one day at a time. When we release our parents from responsibility for our actions today, we become free to make healthful decisions as actors, not reactors. We progress from hurting, to healing, to helping. We awaken to a sense of wholeness we never knew was possible.

By attending these meetings on a regular basis, you will come to see parental alcoholism or family dysfunction for what it is: a disease that infected you as a child and continues to affect you as an adult. You will learn to keep the focus on yourself in the here and now. You will take responsibility for your own life and supply your own parenting.

You will not do this alone. Look around you and you will see others who know how you feel. We will love and encourage you no matter what. We ask you to accept us just as we accept you.

This is a spiritual program based on action coming from love. We are sure that as the love grows inside you, you will see beautiful changes in all your relationships, especially with your Higher Power, yourself, and your parents.

The ACA Twelve Steps

1. We admitted we were powerless over the effects of alcoholism or other family dysfunction, that our lives had become unmanageable.

2. Came to believe that a Power greater than ourselves could restore us to sanity.

3. Made a decision to turn our will and our lives over to the care of God as we understand God.

4. Made a searching and fearless moral inventory of ourselves.

5. Admitted to God, to ourselves, and to another human being the exact nature of our wrongs.

6. Were entirely ready to have God remove all these defects of character.

7. Humbly asked God to remove our shortcomings.

8. Made a list of all persons we had harmed and became willing to make amends to them all.

9. Made direct amends to such people wherever possible, except when to do so would injure them or others.

10. Continued to take personal inventory and when we were wrong promptly admitted it.

11. Sought through prayer and meditation to improve our conscious contact with God, as we understand God, praying only for knowledge of God's will for us and the power to carry that out.

12. Having had a spiritual awakening as the result of these Steps, we tried to carry this message to others who still suffer, and to practice these principles in all our affairs.

The Twelve Steps are adapted and reprinted with permission of Alcoholics Anonymous World Services, Inc.

The Twelve Traditions of ACA

1. Our common welfare should come first; personal recovery depends on ACA unity.

2. For our group purpose there is but one ultimate authority – a loving God as expressed in our group conscience. Our leaders are but Trusted Servants; they do not govern.

3. The only requirement for membership in ACA is a desire to recover from the effects of growing up in an alcoholic or otherwise dysfunctional family.

4. Each group is autonomous except in matters affecting other groups or ACA as a whole. We cooperate with all other Twelve Step programs.

5. Each group has but one primary purpose – to carry its message to the adult child who still suffers.

6. An ACA group ought never endorse, finance, or lend the ACA name to any related facility or outside enterprise, lest problems of money, property, and prestige divert us from our primary purpose.

7. Every ACA group ought to be fully self-supporting, declining outside contributions.

8. Adult Children of Alcoholics should remain forever nonprofessional, but our service centers may employ special workers.

9. ACA, as such, ought never be organized, but we may create service boards or committees directly responsible to those they serve.

10. Adult Children of Alcoholics has no opinion on outside issues; hence the ACA name ought never be drawn into public controversy.

11. Our public relations policy is based on attraction rather than promotion; we maintain personal anonymity at the level of press, radio, TV, films, and other public media.

12. Anonymity is the spiritual foundation of all our Traditions, ever reminding us to place principles before personalities.

The Twelve Traditions are adapted and reprinted with permission of Alcoholics Anonymous World Service Inc.